Copyright © 2012 Shanghai Press and Publishing Development Company

This book is edited and designed by the Editorial Committee of *Cultural China* series

Managing Directors: Wang Youbu, Xu Naiqing
Executive Editor: Yang Xinci
Editor (Chinese): Zhang Wei
Editors (English): Zhang Yicong, Yang Xiaohe

Compiled by Yang Tianwen
Translated with notes by Tony Blishen

Design Consultant: Diane Davies
Designer: Wang Wei
Cover Image: Getty Images

ISBN: 978-1-60220-134-7

Address any comments about *The Art of Attainment* to:
Better Link Press
99 Park Ave
New York, NY 10016
USA

or

Shanghai Press and Publishing Development Company
F 7 Donghu Road, Shanghai, China (200031)
Email: comments_betterlinkpress@hotmail.com

Printed in China by Shenzhen Donnelley Printing Co., Ltd.

1 3 5 7 9 10 8 6 4 2

THE ART OF ATTAINMENT

Quotations from Chinese Wisdom

谋
略

COMPILED BY YANG TIANWEN
TRANSLATED WITH NOTES BY TONY BLISHEN

Better Link Press

Contents

Foreword   7

Chapter I
The Maintenance of the State   11
  People as the Basis   11
  Benevolent Government   14
  Enacting the Law   17
  Implementing the Law   19
  Virtue amongst Officials   22
  Effective Administration   26
  Reform   30

Chapter II
Management   33
  Knowledge of People   33
  The Search for Talent   36
  Skill in Appointment   39
  Wisdom   42
  Caution   46

Accepting Advice   49
Seizing Opportunity   51
Forecasting and Preparation   55
Limits   58

Chapter III
Warfare and Strategy   60
  On War   60
  On Command   64
  On Attack   67
  On Warfare   73

Notes on Sources   77

Dynasties in Chinese History   107

Foreword

This second volume of quotations moves on from the area of the principles of personal behavior and of relationships covered in the first volume to an environment where the skills needed to attain an objective are deployed at all levels, from the purely individual, such as judgment of character, to wider areas such as the conduct of government, management, and warfare.

All these topics are grouped under the single Chinese phrase *moulue*. This is a term so broad in meaning that no really satisfactory English translation exists. It can include almost any action undertaken in pursuit of an aim. It covers a spectrum of meaning from stratagem to strategy in its widest sense. But taken as a whole, the quotations themselves also suggest a level of meaning which carries an underlying sense of the futility of policy or action which lacks a moral basis or does not promote the welfare of those affected. Thus, in government, a matter which was the principal concern of many of the early Chinese philosophers (who, in most cases, earned their living as advisers to rulers), the support of the people and harmony between ruler and the ruled are regarded as essential to the well ordered and hence harmonious state. This sense can extend even to warfare where a victory achieved by stratagem without casualties is more desirable than one won by sheer slaughter.

The sources from which these quotations have been drawn differ little from those in the first volume except in areas such as warfare where they have been drawn additionally from some major early military treatises such as Sun Wu's *Art of War* (*Sunzi Bingfa*) and *The Six Secret Teachings on the Way of Strategy* (*Tai Gong Liu Tao*).

There are notes on sources at the end of the volume. As with the first volume, the task of translating and preparing the notes has been eased by the existence of the internet which has provided instant access to texts and reliable works of reference particularly in Chinese. Material on the sources of Chinese history and literature is now more widely accessible than it has ever been. Chinese is its own Latin and Greek and thus, despite developments in grammatical structure and changes in meaning, has an accessible continuity denied to many other languages.

The vast scope of this selection of quotations from nearly 200 sources covering 2,000 years of Chinese history reflects the breadth and depth of the compiler Mr Yang Tianwen's learning, something that I have come to respect as I have worked on the translations. I have also come to admire the efficiency, dedication and unrivalled bilingual correspondence skills of my editor Miss Zhang Yicong as well as the research skills and support of Miss Yang Xiaohe and other colleagues at the Better Link Press.

Tony Blishen

Chapter I
The Maintenance of the State

People as the Basis

The people are the foundation of the state; if the foundations are firm the state will be tranquil.
— *Classic of History*

The sages of themselves were without purpose, but derived their purpose from the people.
— *Li Er: Laozi*

To rule the people from above speak gently below, to lead from the front, put self behind.
— *Ibid.*

The rule of the enlightened king encompasses the world but appears not of his doing. He provides for all that lives though the people are unaware of it. His merits are not blazoned abroad. The people rejoice in the achievement as their own and acquire virtue insensibly.
— *Zhuang Zhou: Zhuangzi*

A state cannot stand without the confidence of the people.
— *Confucius: Analects*

Magnanimity will win all mankind, diligence will win merit and fairness bring joy.
— *Ibid.*

Treasure the people, then the land, and the ruler least of all.
— *Meng Ke: Mencius*

To win their hearts: give in plenty what they desire and avoid what they do not. That is all.
— *Ibid.*

The affairs of the people are not to be trifled with.
— *Ibid.*

To gain the strength of the people is fortunate, to have their support brings might, to secure their good opinion wins esteem. To hold all three is to have all, to lose all three is to lose all.
— *Xun Kuang: Xunzi*

The ruler is a boat and the people are the water. The boat can float but the water may capsize it.
— *Ibid.*

The world does not belong to one man alone, the world is for all.
— *Lü Buwei: Lü's Spring and Autumn Annals*

A minister should regard it as an achievement to benefit the people but as a crime to impoverish them.
— *Jia Yi: New Essays*

Take responsibility for mistakes upon oneself and
learn caution; give credit for virtue to the people and
they will rejoice.
— *Guan Zhong: Guanzi*

Take account of the strength of the people and there
is nothing that cannot be achieved. Do not force the
unwilling and they will not cheat.
— *Ibid.*

Nurse the people so that the nation may prosper.
— *Zuo Qiuming: Chronicle of Zuo*

The ruler puts the people first but the people put food
first.
— *Ban Gu: Book of Han*

A ruler should regard the welfare of the people as the
core of the state and learning as its foundation.
— *Wang Fu: Discourse of a Man Concealed*

Wealth needs derive from the people, strength
depends upon their effort, renown upon their power,
fortune grows from them, virtue must wait on them
and righteousness must be promoted by them.
— *Chen Shou: Records of Three Kingdoms*

Maintenance of the realm depends upon munificent
virtue and not upon trivial benefit.
— *Ibid.*

If the people are at peace they will take joy in their
lives. If not, they will take death lightly. If they take
death lightly then nothing can be achieved.
— *Chen Zi'ang: Critical Matters of State and Army*

When the people have enough their thoughts turn to peace.
— *Liu Yuxi*

To lose the people for the sake of gain is not the act of
a wise man.
— *Su Shi*

Power without virtue, however fierce, cannot
intimidate the people. Nor can intelligence that lacks
morality secure their acquiescence.
— *Ibid.*

Benevolent Government

The people lack a sense of direction; only direction
will ensure virtuous government.
— *Classic of History*

To bring peace to the people is a blessing, a blessing
which they will embrace.
— *Ibid.*

Do not harm the defenseless or abandon the hopeless.
— *Ibid.*

Where there is virtue there are people, where there
are people there is land, where there is land there is
wealth and where there is wealth there is revenue.
— *Book of Rites*

A tyrannical government is fiercer by far than a tiger.
— *Ibid.*

The righteous will receive succor and the unjust will
not. Those without succor will be abandoned even by

their family but those with it will receive the favor of heaven.
— *Meng Ke: Mencius*

Extend respect for the old to all who are old and love for the young to the young of all and heaven will be within your grasp.
— *Ibid.*

Make it your pleasure to make the people joyful and the people will rejoice with you; take care for the anxieties of the people and your cares will become theirs. Never has a ruler failed thus.
— *Ibid.*

Govern well and the people will bestow their love and die for those that rule them.
— *Ibid.*

If the ruler is benevolent there will be none who are not, if the ruler is just there will be none who are not, if the ruler is righteous there will be none who are not, thus with a righteous ruler the state will be stable.
— *Ibid.*

If the ruler loves the people there is peace, if he nurtures the land there is prosperity, but if either is lacking the state will fail.
— *Xun Kuang: Xunzi*

Where justice prevails over personal advantage there is order, where advantage defeats justice there is confusion.
— *Ibid.*

As heaven and earth have neither self nor partiality
and as the sun and moon shine upon all, so should
the character of the ruler.
— *Guan Zhong: Guanzi*

Eat but know the hunger of others, be warm but
know of their cold, take your ease but know of their toil.
— *The Spring and Autumn Annals of Minister Yan Ying*

Benefit stands upon righteousness and avarice is
the root of hatred; there can be no benefit without
righteousness and unsuppressed avarice breeds hatred.
— *Guoyu*

To rule the people there is nothing better than justice.
— *The School Sayings of Confucius*

The benevolent love all things and the wise are
prepared for disaster. How can a state exist without
these two?
— *Sima Qian: Record of History*

Benevolence needs not martial spirit and justice needs
not power.
— *Ban Gu: Book of Han*

Trifling benefit is the enemy of true magnanimity.
— *Wu Jing: Outline of Affairs during the Zhenguan
Reign of the Tang Dynasty*

The skilled ruler gives ease to the people with pleasure
itself. The unskilled reserves pleasure for his own
enjoyment.
— *Ibid.*

Enacting the Law

Punishment lies in the hope of not having to punish.
— *Classic of History*

Government is the application of law.
— *Xun Yue: The Mirror of History*

The rule of law is the life of the people and the basis of the state.
— *Shang Yang: The Book of Lord Shang*

Show the road to execution but open the gate to reward.
— *Guan Zhong: Guanzi*

The law does not favor the noble, nor custom the evildoer.
— *Han Fei: Han Feizi*

When government is appropriate to the times the people are united and the virtuous are willing.
— *Xun Kuang: Xunzi*

The law has no greater merit than the prevention of personal advantage.
— *Shen Dao: Shenzi*

The law is the best path towards the unity of the people.
— *Han Fei: Han Feizi*

To abandon regulation for mere skill and the law for mere knowledge is the road to disorder.
— *Ibid.*

The law is to guide the people and punishment is to prevent crime.
— *Sima Qian: Record of History*

If the mesh is large the prey will escape, if the law is loose then crime will leak, if crime leaks then people will become feckless and disregard the law.
— *Huan Kuan: Debates on Salt and Iron*

Establish law and the people will not transgress; issue edicts and the people will obey.
— *Ban Gu: Book of Han*

Law restrains the violent and supports the weak to make crime difficult to commit but easy to avoid.
— *Ibid.*

Propriety prevents before the act and the law after it.
— *Ibid.*

The edicts of the state must be simple.
— *Wu Jing: Outline of Affairs during the Zhenguan Reign of the Tang Dynasty*

All law is of necessity defective in the beginning.
— *Han Yu*

The law is established from above but becomes custom below.
— *Su Zhe*

The law proceeds from benevolence but manifests in righteousness.
— *Su Shi*

If man takes precedence over the law then the law becomes an empty vessel, if the law takes precedence

over man then man becomes superfluous. When there is no conflict between man and the law then the world will be at peace.
— *Ibid.*

Each law breeds its own malpractice, that is the way of it, but not to establish laws for fear of malpractice has yet to be regarded as right.
— *Lü Kun: Lamentations*

Implementing the Law

Heave's net is wide but nothing escapes it.
— *Li Er: Laozi*

Forgive error however great, punish fault however small.
— *Classic of History*

Be restrained in sentence but generous in reward.
— *Ibid.*

To avoid excess in anger and in joy, that is how the law overcomes self interest.
— *Xun Kuang: Xunzi*

When punishment fits the crime that is stability, when it does not that is disorder.
— *Ibid.*

Do not harm the innocent or release the guilty and the people will not doubt.
— *The School Sayings of Confucius*

Where there is true merit reward those however distant or lowly; where there is guilt punish those

however close or beloved.
— *Han Fei: Han Feizi*

Fear not a world without law but fear that there is law which is not applied.
— *Huan Kuan: Debates on Salt and Iron*

To reward the undeserving is disorder, to find the unknowing guilty is sheer cruelty.
— *The Spring and Autumn Annals of Minister Yan Ying*

To forbid but yet not to lead by example will not secure the obedience of the people.
— *Ibid.*

The nobility should not escape punishment nor the humble be deprived of reward.
— *Ibid.*

Curb one's own desires and the people will prosper, listen justly and they will be peaceful.
— *Ibid.*

An official does not favor his friends nor is the law lenient to his intimates.
— *Shen Dao: Shenzi*

The law is the instrument of all. Those who uphold it and who treat all far and near as one act correctly, thus none will dare to rely upon it and yet transgress.
— *Sima Guang: Comprehensive Mirror to Aid in Government*

Those skilled in government do not reward lavishly or punish excessively.
— *Zuo Qiuming: Chronicle of Zuo*

When the law fails it is because of those in power.
— *Sima Qian: Record of History*

Not to reward when it is deserved is to fail the
aspirations and doubt the ability of the virtuous;
not to punish when it is deserved is to encourage
contempt for the law and allow evildoers to continue
in their ways.
— *Xu Gan: Balanced Discourses*

To reward insufficiently is to discourage virtue and to
punish insufficiently is to encourage evil.
— *Xun Yue: The Mirror of History*

Reward to encourage merit, punish to prevent
treachery.
— *Zhuge Liang: Sixteen Strategies*

Punishment is not for the sake of severity alone but
for the prevention of evil.
— *Guo Zuo*

A ruler does not reward those who labor for his
personal gain and does not punish those who bear
him personal ill will.
— *Zuo Qiuming: Chronicle of Zuo*

Not to seek talent from far and wide and not to apply
the law to the rich and powerful, is to hinder the
conduct of affairs and leave evil unpunished.
— *Sima Guang: Comprehensive Mirror to Aid in
Government*

Give a hearing to all who feel injustice and give
consolation to the dead.
— *Su Zhe*

To reward where there is doubt is to spread benevolence; not to punish where there is doubt is prudence.
— *Su Shi*

When writs do not run and forbidding lacks effect, rogues will flourish unchecked and good folk swallow their tears.
— *Liang Zhangju*

Virtue amongst Officials

The Heavens, the Earth, the Sun and Moon are without self-interest. Emulate them in striving for the benefit of all and they will become the three principles of selflessness.
— *Book of Rites*

Where there is neither partiality nor cliques, the way of the ruler will flourish.
— *Classic of History*

Labor each day without thought of ease.
— *Ibid.*

Do not despise those below or curry favor with those above.
— *Book of Rites*

Justice enlightens, partiality obscures, and honesty informs, but falsehood stifles, integrity ennobles and flattery confuses.
— *Xun Kuang: Xunzi*

Incorruptibility is called justice.
— *The Spring and Autumn Annals of Minister Yan Ying*

Do not suppress talent to conceal the superiority
of others or oppress inferiors in order to toady to
superiors.
— *Ibid.*

An official must keep his word.
— *Mo Di: Mozi*

A roof may leak below but must be repaired from
above.
— *Zhuge Liang: Sixteen Strategies*

Administration is rectitude and so should rectify
malpractice.
— *Zhang Jiuling*

As enlightenment shines upon all, so is justice
impartial.
— *Wu Jing: Outline of Affairs during the Zhenguan
Reign of the Tang Dynasty*

There is no more to administration than to correct
oneself and to seek the principles of all things.
— *Yan Zhenqing*

To be an official is to serve the people.
— *Liu Zongyuan*

The cares of those in grave office must be deep and
the sense of responsibility of those in high office must
be wide.
— *Wang Anshi*

In a crisis, hold to one's purpose.
— *Su Shi*

One who leads officials must be incorruptible, careful and diligent.
— *Pei Songzhi: Commentaries on Chen Shou's Records of Three Kingdoms*

If an official is just then he is incorruptible.
— *Qian Qi*

Frugality and incorruptibility lead to unwearied effectiveness.
— *Dai Zhen*

Being an official saps the will.
— *Zhu Xi, Lü Zuqian: Reflections on Things at Hand*

Loss of virtue in an official is worse by far than a fierce fire.
— *Classic of History*

Where virtue is lacking but position is high, where wisdom is lacking but schemes are grand and where ability is lacking but responsibility is great, little is achieved.
— *Book of Changes*

Greed defeats the law and indulgence damages morality.
— *Zuo Qiuming: Chronicle of Zuo*

States fail through the iniquity of officials. Officials lose virtue through corruption.
— *Ibid.*

No intention is worse than to oppress the people, no action is worse than to harm them.
— *The Spring and Autumn Annals of Minister Yan Ying*

When there is trouble above there is cheating below, when affairs above are burdensome there is argument below, when there is disturbance above there is disquiet below and when there is avarice above there is looting below.
— *Liu An: Huainanzi*

When officials are upright and without self interest society is in balance and without complaint, the law is open and ministers impartial.
— *Ibid.*

Lack of sincerity above breeds disloyalty below and lack of harmony both above and below causes danger even in peace.
— *Liu Xiang: Garden of Stories*

Self-seeking causes uncontrollable discontent and this damages the integrity of the state.
— *Xun Yue: The Mirror of History*

The disease of officialdom is cruelty that is hidden, corruption that is invisible and negligence that does not seem so.
— *Zhou Shouchang*

Those who disregard the repute of the ruler, or the national good, and who conspire for their own ends are traitors.
— *Xun Kuang: Xunzi*

To regard ruthlessness as efficiency, self-interest as public good, oppression as energy and fawning as loyalty is a betrayal of the nation.
— *Xun Yue: The Mirror of History*

Taking incompetence as simple government, personal honesty as incorruptible administration and rigid adherence to custom as following regulations is like taking one's ease in the doorway and allowing juniors to take matters into their own hands.
— *Liu Yuxi*

An official who stands aside in order to suit his own interest should be dismissed.
— *Bao Zheng*

Effective Administration

Indecision confounds planning and idleness is the ruin of government.
— *Classic of History*

Instruction without lecture and the benefits of inaction are rarely seen.
— *Li Er: Laozi*

Worry not that there is not enough but that it is unevenly distributed. Worry not that there are too few people but that there is instability.
— *Confucius: Analects*

Now taut, now relaxed, that was the way of the rule of kings Wen and Wu of the Zhou dynasty.
— *Book of Rites*

Matters of state should be discussed openly.
— *Ibid.*

A ruler chooses ministers, sets out laws and establishes a purpose to guide and illumine and then to weigh in judgment.
— *Xun Kuang: Xunzi*

The enlightened ruler sets out the grand design but the stupid becomes involved in detail. If the ruler implements the grand design the details will follow but if he implements the details confusion will follow.
— *Ibid.*

Events take place everywhere but the crux is at the center.
— *Han Fei: Han Feizi*

Severity and leniency go hand in hand but government is through harmony.
— *Zuo Qiuming: Chronicle of Zuo*

Govern with the well-being of the people at heart, administer with principle and the rule of law will prevail.
— *Stratagems of the Warring States*

If those above are not arrogant and those below without anxiety, if there is timely vigilance and no opportunity is lost then there will be no disaster.
— *Book of Changes*

Affairs are born of thought, succeed through effort and fail through arrogance.
— *Guan Zhong: Guanzi*

If the crooked cannot be straightened at the center, it can never be straightened.
— *Dong Zhongshu*

Measure income to set expenditure.
— *Book of Rites*

Do not praise beyond merit or criticize beyond defect.
— *Wang Chong: Discourses Weighed in the Balance*

Government is like playing a stringed instrument; if the long strings are too taut the short ones will snap.
— *Liu Xiang: Garden of Stories*

To know that to give is also to receive is the pearl of the wisdom of government.
— *Sima Qian: Record of History*

Both sincerity and stratagem can garner advice. Where others excel appear unable, treat people as your own, heed criticism as if it were a favorable current and respond to events as swiftly as an echo.
— *Ban Biao*

As the fragrance of soup lies in its mixing, so the strength of those above and below lies in mutual aid.
— *Chen Shou: Records of Three Kingdoms*

Ministers regard skill in affairs as strength, rulers regard reward and punishment as strength.
— *Liu Shao: Records of People*

The virtuous ruler distinguishes the extraordinary from the ordinary and selects all the talents. He does not keep matters in his own hands.
— *Ibid.*

Over-correction of error leads to trickery.
— *Chen Shou: Records of Three Kingdoms*

To seek a tree's growth attend to its roots, to lengthen
a river's flow dredge its source.
— *Wei Zheng: Memorial to Emperor Taizong*

Internal caution and excessive concern cripples
outward government; slavish adherence to form stifles
initiative.
— *Bai Juyi: On the Conduct of a Minister*

Be prominent in love of virtue and a ruler may
govern, be prominent in hatred of evil and the rogues
will retreat.
— *Wu Jing: Outline of Affairs during the Zhenguan
Reign of the Tang Dynasty*

Where reason causes disorder it is because reason has
not been put into practice: where disorder leads to
reason it is because disorder can lead to caution.
— *Lu Zhi*

Wisdom enables planning, talent enhances
accomplishment, loyalty serves the state, and
generosity comforts the people.
— *Han Yu: Inscription in Memory of Liu Zongyuan*

To govern you must perceive cause and effect.
— *Han Yu*

See the whole and ignore trifling detail.
— *Su Xun*

Government is about reality.
— *Su Zhe*

Some difficult words should be kept and some easy
advantages rejected.
— *Su Shi*

If there is a straightforward plan above there can
be no misunderstanding below and all will be
accomplished without difficulty.
— *Li Gang*

There are three causes which determine success or
failure: lack of economic power, lack of military
strength and incompetent officials.
— *Su Shi*

Reform

The law turns with the times and thus governs,
government suits the age and thus achieves.
— *Han Fei: Han Feizi*

Government without law is disorder, blind adherence
to the law is stupidity. Stupidity and disorder are no
support to the nation. The age moves with the times
and so should the law.
— *Lü Buwei: Lü's Spring and Autumn Annals*

The wise enact law and the ignorant obey; the worthy
develop the law but the unworthy adhere rigidly to
the old.
— *Shang Yang: The Book of Lord Shang*

The three dynasties each governed with different rites
but govern they did; the five hegemons each ruled

with different law but rule they did.
— *Ibid.*

To be oneself one does not rely upon others, to
regulate the law one does not cling to the past.
— *Stratagems of the Warring States*

The age moves with the times and the law with it, just
as a skilled doctor adjusts his medicine to the illness.
If the symptoms change and the treatment does not,
then those who were to be long lived die early.
— *Lü Buwei: Lü's Spring and Autumn Annals*

For the law to profit the people it need not be ruled
by antiquity; for matters to be well managed they
need not follow the past.
— *Liu An: Huainanzi*

Do not follow the established law but seek to know
upon what grounds it was established. Those grounds
move with the times.
— *Ibid.*

If two stringed instruments are not in tune, then they
must be re-strung.
— *Ban Gu: Book of Han*

To take delight in the old and to avoid the new is
weakness.
— *Han Yu*

Reform is a great undertaking that has its time and
place and talents. Only if it is implemented with
thought and care will there be no regrets on the
morrow.
— *Cheng Hao, Cheng Yi: Collection of the Two Chengs*

To stick with the past in idleness and inaction may by chance achieve peace for a while but it cannot be lasting.
— *Wang Anshi*

If matters are not to stagnate then reason must value change and adaptability.
— *Song History*

The law is the instrument of all and reforms the common principle.
— *Liang Qichao*

Chapter II
Management

Knowledge of People

From knowledge of people comes the wisdom to appoint officials.
— *Classic of History*

The fault in appraising a horse is to see that it is thin but not to recognize its talent; the fault in appraising officials is to see their poverty but not to recognize their skill.
— *Sima Qian: Record of History*

The official of character may lack accomplishment and the accomplished official may lack character.
— *Chen Shou: Records of Three Kingdoms*

To be without merit but to boast, that is third class; to have merit and to boast, that is second class; to have merit and yet not to boast, that is first class. To be stupid but eager to achieve, that is third class; to possess talent and to proclaim it, that is second class;

to combine talent with humility, that is first class.
To allow oneself liberties but to be strict with others,
that is third class; to be strict with others and with
oneself, that is second class; to be strict with oneself
but liberal with others, that is first class.
— *Liu Shao: Records of People*

Of all the characteristics of man, balance is the
most esteemed. Balance must be just so that it may
command the five talents and meet the demands of
change.
— *Ibid.*

The man of quality achieves what others cannot, thus
he wins fame for modesty in success and reputation
for integrity in times of difficulty.
— *Ibid.*

Limited talent is of one flavor only: good for officials
but useless for rulers.
— *Ibid.*

It is easy to recognize the good in others like oneself
but difficult to see it in those who are not.
— *Ibid.*

Those who take jade for stone may well take stone for
jade, and those who mistake talent for stupidity may
just as easily mistake stupidity for talent.
— *Ge Hong: Baopuzi (The Master Who Embraces
Simplicity)*

Understanding without courage is perception without
decision; courage without understanding defies reason

and is inopportune.
— *Ji Kang*

Those who devote themselves to minor details will never achieve fame; those who cannot stomach minor humiliations will never become great.
— *Sima Qian: Record of History*

The small man's abilities are shallow but his intentions large and his effort weak for the task he seeks. Hence he often falls by the wayside.
— *Huan Kuan: Debates on Salt and Iron*

The overcautious will never succeed and the unrestrained will never be accepted.
— *Liu An: Huainanzi*

Those who dare to be great traitors must possess talent beyond the ordinary and the ability to charm their superiors.
— *Wang Fu: Discourse of a Man Concealed*

Be detailed in thought but grand in aspiration; be quick of wit but upright in character; be versatile in ability but straightforward in affairs.
— *Liu An: Huainanzi*

Flowery speech and winning ways are seldom accompanied by virtue.
— *Confucius: Analects*

The stupid and ignorant boast of their abilities and exalt their own talents.
— *Wu Jing: Outline of Affairs during the Zhenguan Reign of the Tang Dynasty*

The darkened mind illuminates nothing and suspects everything.
— *Ibid.*

Only in danger can one recognize heroes.
— *Du Fu*

Talent is only apparent when used.
— *Chen Liang*

The taciturn are not necessarily stupid, nor the wordy wise; the contradictory are not necessarily perverse nor the obedient loyal.
— *Lu Zhi*

The Search for Talent

Seek perfection in no man.
— *Confucius: Analects*

One word may ruin a plan but one man may settle a nation.
— *Book of Rites*

Honesty first and then ability.
— *Xun Kuang: Xunzi*

Wisdom with modesty—that is talent.
— *Ibid.*

In a nation without peace and a populace without rule it will be well with talent but disaster without.
— *Liu Xiang: Garden of Stories*

There is strength in able officials and disaster without them.
— *Sima Qian: Record of History*

The basis of government is the appointment of talent; the function of administration is the eradication of evil.
— *Fan Ye: Book of Later Han*

First there was Bo Le the connoisseur of horses and then there was the thousand mile horse.
— *Han Yu*

In antiquity, the employment of talent was not on the basis of standing. Impoverished scholars with talent were appointed and the talented sons of high officials were also employed.
— *Su Xun*

If you are not open-minded and receptive, how then can you acquire talent!
— *Wang Anshi*

Do not fear that the world so wide lacks talent, fear only the lack of the skill to use it.
— *Bao Zheng*

To be bound by precedent narrows choice, to abandon precedent widens it.
— *Ouyang Xiu*

In government the employment of people is not solely of one kind, hence the appointment of officials should not be confined to one sort.
— *Ibid.*

Good officials may be easy to find but difficult to make demands of, easy to engage but difficult to keep.
— *Jia Yi: New Essays*

No generation lacks outstanding talent, it is just that it is left in the wilderness!
— *Zuo Si*

If the talent fits the bill do not enquire too closely; if knowledge suffices the scheme what matters the small defect?
— *Liu Zhou: Liuzi*

If those who are generally acclaimed are considered as talented and those who are generally condemned are regarded as lacking talent, then those in the majority will progress and those in the minority will not.
— *The Six Secret Teachings on the Way of Strategy*

To seek talent by avoiding defects but forgetting the strengths is like writing in the air or emptying a river to seek a road. It can never succeed.
— *Liu Zhou: Liuzi*

As to talent, breadth of experience first and then knowledge.
— *Su Shi*

The promises of a thousand are not worth the plain word of a single man of quality.
— *Ibid.*

The loyal minister who dares speak his mind is a jewel of state.
— *Sima Guang*

People do not consider self-regard as a virtue.
— *Su Shi*

Skill in Appointment

There can be no two ways about the appointment of
talent or hesitation over the eradication of evil.
— *Classic of History*

In making appointments the enlightened ruler
does not surround himself with flattery or allow
prejudice to hold sway. He appoints on ability and
does not encourage the lack of it. He appoints skill
and not incapacity. This is the policy for making
appointments.
— *The Spring and Autumn Annals of Minister Yan Ying*

A ruler has three concerns: that character should
match position, that salary should match achievement
and that ability should match appointment.
— *Guan Zhong: Guanzi*

Those who do not command the confidence of the
people should not be appointed to high office.
— *Ibid.*

To hold high office without virtue is to foist evil upon
the people.
— *Meng Ke: Mencius*

There can be no respect without virtue and no official
post without ability.
— *Xun Kung: Xunzi*

Where virtue does not match appointment the disaster will be cruel. Where ability does not match position the calamity will be great.
— *Wang Fu: Discourse of a Man Concealed*

Respect worth and employ the able. With the outstanding in office, the worthy will rejoice and support the reign.
— *Meng Ke: Mencius*

Do not wait upon precedence to promote the able, do not wait upon necessity to dismiss the incompetent.
— *Xun Kuang: Xunzi*

Do not ignore the faults of those you like or the achievements of those you dislike.
— *Zuo Qiuming: Chronicle of Zuo*

In promoting afar do not neglect your enemies, in promoting within do not neglect your friends.
— *Ibid.*

The more able the evil the greater the harm.
— *Wu Jing: Outline of Affairs during the Zhenguan Reign of the Tang Dynasty*

The employment of the upright is an encouragement to the virtuous, but employment of the wicked advances the evil.
— *Ibid.*

The faults of the wise are less than the virtues of the ignorant; the deficiencies of the able are less than the adequacies of the many.
— *Liu An: Huainanzi*

With office there comes appraisal, with appraisal there
comes punishment and reward.
— *Su Xun*

Reward according to achievement and allocate tasks
according to ability.
— *Han Fei: Han Feizi*

Perfection in ability and conduct is rare and
where there is advantage there is also fault. Where
advantage repairs fault there are none who may not
be employed, but where fault attracts blame there are
none who may escape dismissal.
— *Lu Zhi*

Strict selection will attract talent and proper reward
will encourage the able.
— *Ouyang Xiu*

The master carpenter casts aside no wood—boats and
carriages need different kinds.
— *Cao Zhi*

A square peg will not fit a round hole and straight
wood will not make a wheel. Gauge each material
according to its use, for use against its nature brings
difficulty.
— *Wei Yingwu*

Use a cock to crow at dawn and a dog to catch rats.
Use all according to ability and the world will be well.
— *Han Fei: Han Feizi*

Those skilled in the grand design should not be
burdened with trivial detail; those of little wisdom

should not be entrusted with grave affairs.
— *Liu An: Huainanzi*

Wisdom

To see clearly is to perceive, to listen to virtue is to understand.
— *Classic of History*

Seek neither haste nor petty advantage. Haste leads nowhere and petty advantage hinders achievement.
— *Confucius: Analects*

The sages practise benign inaction and teach without instructing. They do not commence but follow nature, they nurture it rather than possess it, they promote it rather than exploit it, they accomplish rather than occupy.
— *Li Er: Laozi*

Heaven's way seeks advantage without harm; the sages seek existence without strife.
— *Ibid.*

Square but without sharp corners, direct but restrained, bright but not blinding.
— *Ibid.*

Do nothing and there is nothing that cannot be done.
— *Ibid.*

Seeking possession brings loss and striving to achieve brings defeat.
— *Wang Bi: Commentaries on Laozi*

Place yourself at the back and you will be in front,
place yourself outside and you will preserve the inside.
— *Ibid.*

It is better to seize the moment than to be wise.
— *Meng Ke: Mencius*

Forcing seedlings to grow is to pull them up; there is
no advantage and much harm.
— *Ibid.*

The whip may be long but it will not reach the horse's belly.
— *Zuo Qiuming: Chronicle of Zuo*

The benevolent should not sever friendship casually
or the wise lightly bear a grudge.
— *Stratagems of the Warring States*

The more you simplify the more you can manage.
— *Xun Kuang: Xunzi*

In the management of affairs the wise consider the
consequences.
— *Ibid.*

Know the distant through the near, the myriad
through the one and the obvious through the hidden.
— *Ibid.*

Feel shame in failure to improve oneself but not in
humiliation; feel shame in being unreliable but not
in lack of reliability in others; feel shame in lack of
ability but not in failure to gain office.
— *Ibid.*

Those with deep cravings are shallow in spirit.
— *Zhuang Zhou: Zhuangzi*

Rid oneself of trivial knowledge and the greater knowledge will be plain to see.
— *Ibid.*

Everyone knows the use of the useful but none the use of the useless.
— *Ibid.*

Gauge its harm, consider its drawbacks.
— *Ibid.*

Secure the advantage, avoid the harm.
— *Ibid.*

The universe possesses a great beauty that is unspoken, the four seasons have virtues that go undiscussed and nature has logic that is not mentioned. For this reason the Magi exist in inaction and sages do not act but follow the course of nature.
— *Ibid.*

Observe to the front but have care for the rear.
— *Record of Rites Compiled by Dai De*

It is not too late to call the dog when you see the rabbit or to repair the fence when the goats have gone.
— *Stratagems of the Warring States*

Enlightenment comes through individuality and through enlightenment one attains the ultimate.
— *Guan Zhong: Guanzi*

Jettison self and observe the law of nature.
— *Ibid.*

The sage fears the miniscule and the ignorant the obvious.
— *Ibid.*

You cannot perceive the whole from the detail or the detail from the whole.
— *Zhuang Zhou*

A little knowledge is a dangerous thing.
— *Liu Xiang: Garden of Stories*

The wisest do not place themselves in danger and then hope for luck, the less wise extract glory from danger and the stupid believe themselves safe in danger and perish thereby.
— *Fan Ye: Book of Later Han*

Advance suggests the possibility of retreat, existence the possibility of destruction and attainment the possibility of failure .
— *Wu Jing: Outline of Affairs during the Zhenguan Reign of the Tang Dynasty*

The wise avoid the headlong rush: when the moment passes the way will still be open.
— *Chen Zi'ang*

In involvement lies confusion; clarity belongs to the onlooker.
— *New Book of Tang*

Light seems brighter in the dark and action is discerned more clearly in tranquility.
— *Su Shi*

The strength of wisdom is swift decision and the strength of courage is action.
— *Ibid.*

The world has none wiser than the wise who can appear stupid.
— *Liu Ji*

Ability and daring spring from knowledge and thus it is that knowledge is difficult to acquire.
— *Li Zhi: Books to Be Burnt*

Each cause spawns its own ills.
— *Hong Zicheng: Vegetable Roots Discourse*

The man of quality succeeds through painstaking endeavor; the mediocrity fails through following the crowd.
— *Wang Fuzhi*

Even the wise can be stupid.
— *Classic of Poetry*

There is difficulty even for the wise and lack of attainment even amongst mystics.
— *Zhuang Zhou: Zhuangzi*

Caution

Care at the last as care at the first prevents disaster.
— *Li Er: Laozi*

Reckon your means before you act and mishaps will be few.
— *Zuo Qiuming: Chronicle of Zuo*

Zi Zhang sought knowledge about preferment. The Master said, "Enquire widely, set aside the doubtful and expound what is left as far as it is reliable and faults will be few; observe widely, set aside what seems perilous and implement the rest. Where speech is without fault and action without regret—there is preferment."
— *Confucius: Analects*

Do not guess, do not jump to conclusions, do not be obstinate and do not be self-willed.
— *Ibid.*

Understanding is easy, but keeping one's own counsel is difficult.
— *Zhuang Zhou: Zhuangzi*

To reach conclusions without checking—that is stupidity.
— *Han Fei: Han Feizi*

The gentleman is cautious about unfounded statements, unverified actions and unheard of schemes.
— *Xun Kuang: Xunzi*

Knowledge is not greater than proper doubt and action itself less important than the need to act without cause for regret.
— *Liu Xiang: Garden of Stories*

Prudence is caution over small things and wisdom is control of the large.
— *Wei Liaozi*

Disaster lies hidden and springs in surprise.
— *Ban Gu: Book of Han*

Do not neglect the insignificant, a little river can sink a boat; do not neglect the small in size, a little insect has a poisonous bite; do not neglect the little man, a little man can betray the nation.
— *Guan Yin Zi*

Neglect of small matters brings great disaster, underestimating a minor enemy brings swift destruction.
— *Liu Ji*

Do not think any offence so trivial that it may be committed or any good deed so small that it need not be performed.
— *Chen Shou: Records of Three Kingdoms*

Light is one extremity of heavy and small is the fount of large; thus dykes collapse because of ant holes and bladders burst from pinpricks.
— *Fan Ye: Book of Later Han*

It is easier to suppress evil at the start and more difficult as it grows. Because people ignore the small they suffer by the large.
— *Ibid.*

Birds fear to perch too low and seek the higher branch, fish fear the shallows and seek the deep, but all are caught through greed for bait.
— *Wu Jing: Outline of Affairs during the Zhenguan Reign of the Tang Dynasty*

To ignore the need for care in time of peace brings woe.
— *Ibid.*

Disaster is an accumulation of tiny mistakes and the wise are often brought down by those they favor.
— *Ouyang Xiu*

Decadence is born of wealth and disaster of neglect.
— *Sima Guang: Comprehensive Mirror to Aid in Government*

Be steadfast in aim, be not eager for petty advantage.
— *Ouyang Xiu*

Misfortune in all matters stems from the miniscule, thus one should beware of cumulative error.
— *Cheng Hao*

People ignore minor defects, hence the causes of major regret.
— *Liu An: Huainanzi*

Accepting Advice

The ancients said, seek opinion from the woodcutters and those who cut grass.
— *Classic of Poetry*

Observe with the eyes of all and there is nothing that is invisible, listen with ears of all and there is nothing that may not be heard, consider with the mind of all and there is nothing that may not be known.
— *The Six Secret Teachings on the Way of Strategy*

Do not stint in criticism of those who share your views.
— *Classic of History*

Act stupidly and on your own and nothing will be achieved.
— *Xun Kuang: Xunzi*

The mouths of the people are the gateway to both misfortune and to fortune.
— *Guoyu*

It is worse by far to gag the people than to dam a river. When the river bursts its banks many suffer, so it is with people. Hence the river is channelled so that its waters may flow, so too should the speech of people.
— *Ibid.*

An enlightened ruler must have three concerns: to hold high office yet not to be told of his own defects, to become arrogant through his own achievements, and to receive the best advice yet to be unable to act on it.
— *Liu Xiang: Garden of Stories*

Those who appoint advisers need to fear that they may not hear of their own faults.
— *Ban Gu: Book of Han*

The enlightenment of rulers lies in listening and their lack of it in prejudice.
— *Wang Fu: Discourse of a Man Concealed*

Only those who have reason will accept unwelcome advice.
— *Chen Shou: Records of the Three Kingdoms*

There is that which may be plucked from street chatter.
— *Ban Gu: Book of Han*

Those who act alone are isolated and those who refuse advice are secluded.
— *Fan Ye: Book of Later Han*

To act according to a common perception—can it be that there is no broader vision? To implement on the basis of an ordinary scheme—can it be that there is no greater plan?
— *Bai Juyi*

If a ruler listens to the opinions of those below, then ministers cannot stifle them and the feelings of the people will be known above.
— *Wu Jing: Outline of Affairs during the Zhenguan Reign of the Tang Dynasty*

Since antiquity memorials to the throne have been complete and frank. Were they not so they could not attract the attention of the ruler.
— *Ibid.*

To permit mention of the unmentionable opens the way to straight talking.
— *Wang Anshi*

It is easy to be an official but difficult to accept opinion: if accepting opinion is easy, then it is determining its truth that is difficult.
— *Qi Jiguang*

Seizing Opportunity

Act when the time is ripe and rest when it is not. When action and inaction are both in step with the

time, then the future is bright.
— *Book of Changes*

Think well before acting but seize the opportunity.
— *Classic of History*

The gentleman yields when the moment demands it
and proceeds when the time is ripe.
— *Xun Kuang: Xunzi*

The clever man's plan is never better than the right
opportunity.
— *Guan Zhong: Guanzi*

Proceed when the time is ripe and return to a state
of perfection. When it is not, withdraw and wait in
tranquility. This is the road to self-preservation.
— *Zhang Zhou: Zhuangzi*

The sages commanded neither time nor opportunity
but could act in accordance with them. Those who
can act thus will achieve much.
— *Lü Buwei: Lü's Spring and Autumn Annals*

The ease and difficulty of affairs lies not in whether
they are great or small but in timing.
— *Ibid.*

In affairs the sages seemed slack but were eager,
seemed slow but were fast, thus they waited upon
opportunity.
— *Ibid.*

Heaven does not give twice, nor the moment linger.
— *Ibid.*

The gentleman acts upon opportunity and does not wait the day.
— *Book of Changes*

Do not lose opportunity, it will not come again; opportunity offered and not taken brings harm instead.
— *Guoyu*

The sages dwelt in solitude to avoid humiliation, calmly awaiting opportunity.
— *Liu An: Huainanzi*

It is sheer chance that all those in high places are not necessarily talented and sheer mischance that all those in inferior positions are not necessarily stupid.
— *Wang Chong: Discourses Weighed in the Balance*

True principle is always to be esteemed but should be given weight when the time is suitable and implemented when the situation is right.
— *The School Sayings of Confucius*

Better a good year than labor in the fields and better happy chance than loyal service.
— *Sima Qian: Record of History*

Never lose an opportunity; success lies in seizing it swiftly.
— *Chen Shou: Records of the Three Kingdoms*

The sage moves with the times but the common man knows not change.
— *Fan Ye: Book of Later Han*

The great man holds to principle but waits on opportunity.
— *Bai Juyi: Letter to Yuan Zhen*

There are matters that will succeed whether or not the common man can accomplish them, and situations that will fail whether or not a sage may master them.
— *Bai Juyi*

It is difficult to manage the affairs of heaven without first judging its direction.
— *Su Xun*

Success is swiftly snatched and tardiness prevents arrival, hence sages and men of talent prize the fleeting opportunity.
— *Su Shi*

Ease of achievement comes through knowing the mood of the people and strength through perceiving the tendency of the times .
— *Ibid.*

To act before the time is ripe is called impetuosity; impetuosity negates careful consideration and causes doubt above. Failure to seize the opportunity when the time is ripe is called indifference; indifference confounds affairs and negates the will of the ruler.
— *Wang Anshi*

No man can command the direction in which the affairs of heaven move.
— *Chen Liang*

Forecasting and Preparation

There is preparation in all things and with preparation there is no disaster.
— *Classic of History*

If there is one word that is of benefit in the exercise of wisdom it is "preparation."
— *The School Sayings of Confucius*

There is root and branch to everything and start and conclusion to each matter; to know the first and last of all is to approach mastery.
— *Book of Rites*

Success in all things requires preparation, without it there is failure.
— *Ibid.*

To consider matters in advance is called forethought. With forethought there is success.
— *Xun Kuang: Xunzi*

With forethought and early planning, little explanation is required to make meaning clear.
— *Ibid.*

Sudden events cannot be handled by the unprepared mind.
— *Mo Di: Mozi*

The superior man anticipates disaster and takes precautions.
— *Book of Changes*

To prepare for disaster before it strikes prevents it
growing.
— *Guan Zhong: Guanzi*

To consider the problems only after the event is called
tardiness; tardiness accomplishes nothing. To think
of the problems only after disaster strikes is to be
trapped; once trapped disaster cannot be controlled.
— *Xun Kuang: Xunzi*

Disaster overtakes those who cannot read its omens.
— *Guan Zhong: Guanzi*

The stupid cannot envision the finished article but the
wise can anticipate the yet unfinished.
— *Shang Yang: The Book of Lord Shang*

The sages devoted effort to the inchoate and not to
the formed, thus they avoided harm.
— *Liu An: Huainanzi*

The quick and alert are skilled in assessment, the wise
are skilled in preparation.
— *Ibid.*

Were the stupid as prepared as the wise they would be
as accomplished.
— *Ibid.*

In rule through the principles of the classics,
place value upon pre-empting trouble; in military
operations place value upon winning before joining
battle.
— *Ban Gu: Book of Han*

The sages did not wait for illness to appear before curing it, but acted to prevent it; they did not wait for disorder to erupt but acted to suppress it.
— *The Yellow Emperor's Classic of Internal Medicine*

To treat illness only when it presents and to control disorder only when it has broken out is like digging a well only when thirsty or making weapons only after battle is joined. Is that not then too late?
— *Ibid.*

Study of victory and defeat past and present demonstrates that those who saw opportunity and seized it reaped the benefit.
— *Chen Shou: Records of the Three Kingdoms*

Those who plan before they act do well and those who act first and scheme later come to naught.
— *Chen Zi'ang: Memorial to Empress Wu Zetian*

Prior readiness is a permanent national principle.
— *Wu Jing: Outline of Affairs during the Zhenguan Reign of the Tang Dynasty*

Calamity can be nipped in the bud.
— *Ouyang Xiu*

To be able to anticipate the course of events prevents anxiety and allows unflustered action that leads to success.
— *Su Shi*

To plan for trouble in untroubled times prevents anxiety in times of trouble.
— *Su Zhe*

Limits

Knowing when to stop prevents peril.
— *Li Er: Laozi*

Too much is as bad as not enough.
— *Confucius: Analects*

In the large, the limits of morality may not be
crossed; in the little you may to and fro.
— *Ibid.*

In hatred do not part company with reason, in desire
do not outrun affection.
— *Guan Zhong: Guanzi*

Meet change with balance and no more.
— *The Constancy of Laws*

To love appropriately is called humanity, to give
to others appropriately is called righteousness, to
think for others appropriately is called wisdom,
to act appropriately is called fitting and to speak
appropriately is called truth.
— *Shi Jiao: Shizi*

Wine in excess is disorder and joy in excess is grief.
— *Sima Qian: Record of History*

Too hard and it will break, too soft and it will collapse.
— *Ban Gu: Book of Han*

The way of the sages is both liberal and strict, severe
and moderate, yielding and rigid, fierce and yet
benevolent.
— *Liu An: Huainanzi*

What the ancients called the doctrine of the mean, is to implement nothing beyond the laws of nature.
— *Su Shi*

An overabundance of rain is a disaster of nature and overabundant love is a disaster for progeny.
— *Lü Kun: Lamentations*

Chapter III
Warfare and Strategy

On War

Warfare is a profound matter of state. Upon it depend life or death, existence or destruction. Its study cannot be neglected.
— *Sun Wu: Sunzi (The Art of War)*

The state may flourish but there is danger in love of war; the state may be at peace but there is danger in forgetting war.
— *Bai Juyi: The Forest of Stratagems*

The state may always have an army, but there is not always victory in arms; there is always vital ground, but not always superiority in defense.
— *Chen Shou: Records of the Three Kingdoms*

Soldiers are not toys, and playing games leads to loss of power: nor should soldiers be thrown away, that is an invitation to the enemy.
— *Liu Xiang: Garden of Stories*

Weapons are inauspicious and no instrument for a ruler; they are a last resort.
— *Li Er: Laozi*

To use warfare to prevent war; that is permissible.
— *Shang Yang: The Book of Lord Shang*

The enlightened ruler uses warfare to rid the land of harm and shares its fruits with the people.
— *Liu An: Huainanzi*

The crux of warfare is to bring the people to adapt to it.
— *Xun Kuang: Xunzi*

Setting out to war without purpose brings nothing to fruition.
— *Ban Gu: Book of Han*

The purpose of warfare is to suppress violence not to create it.
— *Liu An: Huainanzi*

In war, training comes first.
— *Wu Qi: Wuzi*

The skill in warfare lies in bringing the people to adapt to it.
— *Han Fei: Han Feizi*

Achieving outright victory in battle is not the ultimate skill; achieving the collapse of the enemy without a fight is the ultimate skill.
— *Sun Wu: Sunzi (The Art of War)*

All wars are won by strength in the long term and by morale.
— *Sima's Rules of War*

Weapons are sharp or blunt, victory is not guaranteed.
— *Pei Songzhi: Commentaries on Chen Shou's Records of Three Kingdoms*

A swift victory is better than a long war.
— *Sun Wu: Sunzi (The Art of War)*

It is easier to win a war than to preserve its victory.
— *Wu Qi: Wuzi*

Strength comes from an upright leader and weakness from a crooked one.
— *Zuo Qiuming: Chronicle of Zuo*

Victory may be foreseen but not assumed.
— *Sun Wu: Sunzi (The Art of War)*

Do not hold that the attack will never come but hold to the means to withstand it.
— *Ouyang Xiu: Memorial on Li Zhaoliang's Failure as a General*

How can one permit others to snore alongside one's own bedspace?
— *Yue Ke: Ting Shi*

Without preparation or planning there can be no warfare.
— *Zuo Qiuming: Chronicle of Zuo*

Raising an army from an impoverished land cannot bring certain victory. If victorious there will be many dead. Territory may be won but the state will collapse. These are the disasters of war.
— *Guan Zhong: Guanzi*

Frequent campaigns are the real disaster.
— *Mo Di: Mozi*

War is like a fire: if you do not put down your
weapons, it will consume you.
— *Zuo Qiuming: Chronicle of Zuo*

The ill conduct of war lies in never ending, the skill
lies in concluding it.
— *Wu Jing: Outline of Affairs during the Zhenguan
Reign of the Tang Dynasty*

Endless war impoverishes the people and incessant
campaigning exhausts the troops.
— *Stratagems of the Warring States*

A war of exhaustion to the uttermost always brings
destruction upon oneself.
— *Wu Jing: Outline of Affairs during the Zhenguan
Reign of the Tang Dynasty*

Ignorant involvement in military matters confuses an
army.
— *Sun Wu: Sunzi (The Art of War)*

Both victory and defeat in war lie in politics.
— *Liu An: Huainanzi*

A ruler should not raise an army out of anger nor do
generals go to war in forgiveness. Mobilize only when
it is in the interests of the state.
— *Sun Wu: Sunzi (The Art of War)*

Skill lies only in the achievement of the result, not in
daring to grasp power.
— *Li Er: Laozi*

On Command

A general skilled in warfare is master of the people's destiny and of the nation's fate.
— *Sun Wu: Sunzi (The Art of War)*

If a general issues the wrong order the army can be destroyed and lives lost.
— *Lü Buwei: Lü's Spring and Autumn Annals*

A general who knows not warfare delivers his ruler to the enemy; a ruler who knows not his generals delivers his people to the enemy.
— *Ban Gu: Book of Han*

Rank without arrogance, victory without confusion, worth with modesty and strength with tolerance.
— *Zhuge Liang: The Qualities of a General*

The day a general receives his orders he forgets his family, within the military regime he forgets his relatives but at the drumbeat he must forget his life.
— *Sima Qian: Record of History*

To be a general one must see all and know all oneself. See that which others do not see, know that which others do not know. Seeing what others do not see is called perception and knowing what others do not know is called omniscience. These will assure victory.
— *Liu An: Huainanzi*

To be a general one must first cultivate one's mind.
— *Su Xun: On Schemes*

A general amongst generals must first know reason and then raise the army, must first comprehend

the situation and then join battle and must first understand restraint and then deploy his troops.
— *Ibid.*

Above all, a general must divine his opponent's qualities and examine his talents so that he can deploy his own strengths accordingly.
— *Wu Qi: Wuzi*

When a general is in command of his army there are orders that he may refuse.
— *Sima Qian: Record of History*

Where the general is able but the ruler drives, that is to fetter the army; where the general is incompetent but yet is given a mission, that is to destroy the army.
— *Pei Songzhi: Commentaries on Chen Shou's Records of the Three Kingdoms*

Those who avoid applying the law to their intimates or to the powerful cannot be generals.
— *Guan Zhong: Guanzi*

A skilled commander does not boast of bravery, a skilled fighter is not angered by the enemy, and the skilled victor avoids engagement.
— *Li Er: Laozi*

Those skilled in warfare first avoid the conditions of defeat and then seek the means of victory.
— *Sun Wu: Sunzi (The Art of War)*

Those skilled in warfare never lose an advantage nor let slip an opportunity.
— *The Six Secret Teachings on the Way of Strategy*

To know the outcome before battle is joined; that can be called mastery of warfare.
— *Ban Gu: Book of Han*

Not to take guard and merely to rely on one's strength is to take warfare lightly and brings defeat, but to know one's own weaknesses strengthens planning and brings victory.
— *Su Shi*

Those skilled in warfare are assured in the exploitation of situations. This gives them strength and more.
— *Su Xun: On Schemes*

The famous generals amongst the ancients were masters of the unusual and won battles thereby.
— *Ouyang Xiu: Inscription in Honor of Wang Yanzhang*

To command bodies but not hearts is like acting alone.
— *Guan Zhong: Guanzi*

A general must be the first to take on arduous labor.
— *Wei Liaozi*

Look on soldiers as infants and with them you can go to the ends of the earth. Regard them as a beloved son and with them you can go to death itself.
— *Sun Wu: Sunzi (The Art of War)*

Be not proud in achievement, nor boast, nor be arrogant. Regard achievement as gained despite itself and not for power.
— *Li Er: Laozi*

There is no greater disaster than to underestimate the enemy.
— *Li Er: Laozi*

He who hesitates over his own chess piece will never take his opponent's.
— *Zuo Qiuming: Chronicle of Zuo*

On Attack

Know the enemy and know yourself and there will be little danger in battle.
— *Sun Wu: Sunzi (The Art of War)*

First of all, plan, then negotiate, then go to war. Last and least of all, besiege.
— *Ibid.*

Those skilled in warfare subjugate the enemy without giving battle, take their fortifications without attack and swiftly destroy their nation. Use all means so that the army seizes advantage without pausing. This is the way to plan an offensive.
— *Ibid.*

Those who know when to fight and when not to fight will win, those who know when to use many and when to use few will win, those whose aim is united above and below will win, those who anticipate will defeat those who cannot, and able generals unchecked by their ruler will win.
— *Ibid.*

If you do not thoroughly appreciate the dangers of warfare, you cannot absolutely realize its advantages.
— *Ibid.*

If those who win are not known for wisdom or courage it is because their victories are faultless; faultless because their tactics achieve victory and always put the enemy at a disadvantage.
— *Ibid.*

There are roads which should not be taken, armies that should not be attacked, fortifications that should not be invested, ground that should not be contended and orders from the ruler that should not be accepted.
— *Ibid.*

There is nothing greater than the need for victory, and no greater means than secrecy.
— *The Six Secret Teachings on the Way of Strategy*

True wisdom is not apparent and skilled planning does not show.
— *Ibid.*

Victory without engagement means an army without injury.
— *Ibid.*

Seize the enemy's morale and grasp its general's heart.
— *Sun Wu: Sunzi (The Art of War)*

In war it is better to attack the mind rather than the city, to wage a war of minds rather than of men.
— *Zhuge Liang: Expedition to the South*

Seize first that which they value and they will be at your mercy.
— *Sun Wu: Sunzi (The Art of War)*

Those who preserve the fruits of victory do so by regarding their own strength as weakness.
— *Lie Yukou: Liezi*

The victor wins first and then seeks battle, the defeated fight first and then seek victory.
— *Sun Wu: Sunzi (The Art of War)*

First make oneself impregnable, then wait for the enemy to present an opportunity for victory.
— *Zhao Chongguo: On the Twelve Advantages of Military Farms*

The wise consider both advantage and disadvantage. Consideration of advantage breeds confidence and consideration of disadvantage prevents disaster.
— *Sun Wu: Sunzi (The Art of War)*

In attack rely on planning rather than strength, in engagement rely on knowledge rather than numbers.
— *Ouyang Xiu*

Subtlety, subtlety to the point of formlessness. Mystery, mystery to the point of silence and you will be in command of the enemy.
— *Sun Wu: Sunzi (The Art of War)*

The skill in warfare is to leave the enemy positioned in emptiness, as if grappling with a shadow.
— *Guan Zhong: Guanzi*

An army stands through deception, maneuvers to advantage and concentrates and disperses to change.
— *Sun Wu: Sunzi (The Art of War)*

Meet disorder with order and noise with silence; this is the spirit of discipline.
— *Ibid.*

Those skilled in transformation will not be easily deceived; those knowledgeable in the art will not be alarmed by the unusual.
— *Lu Jia: New Words*

War is the art of cunning; before it starts there should be no excessive secrecy.
— *Pei Songzhi: Commentaries on Chen Shou's Records of the Three Kingdoms*

When a general wishes to defeat the enemy he must assist them, when he wishes to make gains he must encourage them.
— *Stratagems of the Warring States*

When an army is calm it is determined, when it is concentrated it is strong, when it is decisive it is courageous, but when it is uncertain it is doomed and when it is dispersed it is weak.
— *Liu An: Huainanzi*

Victory is always possible. Even if the enemy is many it can be prevented from engaging.
— *Sun Wu: Sunzi (The Art of War)*

When weapons are not sharp and equipment incomplete, it is the same as having no weapons.
— *Guan Zhong: Guanzi*

Those skilled in war do not recruit more than once for a single campaign and do not supply more than twice.
— *Sun Wu: Sunzi (The Art of War)*

Before war husband resources, prior to battle husband one's strength, after battle husband morale and after victory maintain fighting spirit.
— *Su Xun: On Schemes*

A righteous cause inspires soldiers and once inspired they will fight for ever.
— *Ibid.*

You must be able to defend before you can fight, and be able to fight before you can come to terms.
— *Song History*

Those skilled in attack do not exhaust their resources in attacking strongly held fortifications. Those skilled in defense do not exhaust their strength in defending the objectives of enemy attack.
— *Su Xun: On Attack and Defense*

First seize the minds of the enemy and then await signs of weakness.
— *Zuo Quming: Chronicle of Zuo*

Use near to bring the enemy far, use respite to cause the enemy fatigue, use sufficiency to make the enemy hunger: this is the way to marshal ones strength.
— *Sun Wu: Sunzi (The Art of War)*

First like a maiden to disarm the enemy, then like a vanishing hare that he cannot catch.
—*Ibid.*

Those skilled in war avoid the enemy's ardor but attack his lack of vigilance.

— *Ibid.*

Survival can follow a perilous position but life can follow a fatal one.

— *Ibid.*

Do not attack an enemy beneath its banners in war array, nor an army drawn up to give battle: this is the art of maneuver.

— *Ibid.*

Do not obstruct a fleeing army nor seal off a surrounded one.

— *Ibid.*

If you think to live you will die, if you think to die you will live.

— *Wu Qi: Wuzi*

If two armies are evenly matched, the one that grieves will win.

— *Li Er: Laozi*

To think of living on the eve of battle prevents the exertion of all one's strength.

— *Su Shi: Record of the Hall of Thought*

In a long war an army loses its mettle, in a long offensive its strength begins to wane and prolonged warfare exhausts the national treasury. Hence the value of speed.

— *Fan Jun: The Art of the Unexpected*

The small enemy's ability to resist only, becomes the large enemy's prey.
— *Sun Wu: Sunzi (The Art of War)*

On Warfare

All battles are fought face to face but won by stratagem.
— *Sun Wu: Sunzi (The Art of War)*

In war there is nothing beyond face to face combat and stratagem, but the alternation of face to face with stratagem is beyond calculation and resembles an endless cycle. Who can fathom it?
— *Ibid.*

Warfare is deception, so that capability may appear as inability and use as uselessness, the close as distant and the distant as close.
— *Ibid.*

There is no fixed form to warfare just as there is no fixed shape to water. To gain victory through the enemy's own maneuvering is wonderful indeed.
— *Ibid.*

The nature of warfare is a swiftness that leaves the enemy no time to react, thus attack his unreadiness along unexpected routes.
— *Ibid.*

Those skilled in defense conceal themselves in impenetrable ground, those skilled in attack

maneuver in difficult space.
— *Ibid.*

Attack what the enemy cannot hold, hold what the enemy cannot attack.
— *Su Xun: On Attack and Defense*

In warfare you must explore the enemy's strengths and weaknesses and attack his vulnerability.
— *Wu Qi: Wuzi*

Attack where he cannot reach and reach where he cannot foresee.
— *Sun Wu: Sunzi (The Art of War)*

The use of stratagem lies in speed and speed lies in decision.
— *Ouyang Xiu: Inscription in Honor of Wang Yanzhang*

In warfare appear weak but approach with determination, appear weak but assault in strength, withdraw but actually advance, appear in the east but strike in the west.
— *Liu An: Huainanzi*

If a general wishes his opponent to sheath his sword he must let him expand, if he wishes to weaken him he must allow him to strengthen, if he wishes to destroy him, he must allow him to flourish, if he wishes to take him he must concede. This is to achieve the material from the immaterial and use weakness to defeat strength.
— *Li Er: Laozi*

In war, speed even though clumsy is decisive, and dexterity in the long term yet to be seen. It has never

been that protracted warfare has benefited a nation.
— *Sun Wu: Sunzi (The Art of War)*

Dispersal weakens and doubt demoralizes.
— *Wei Liaozi*

Those skilled in warfare first weaken the enemy, and
then attack to achieve twice the victory with half the
means.
— *Liu An: Huainanzi*

Tempt with the offer of advantage, confuse them and
then attack.
— *Sun Wu: Sunzi (The Art of War)*

The enlightened ruler and the wise general will
achieve much if they employ spies of superior
intelligence.
— *Sun Wu: Sunzi (The Art of War)*

Attack with skill and the enemy does not know where
to defend; defend with skill and the enemy does not
know where to attack.
— *Ibid.*

Warfare cannot be foretold: when faced with difficulty
adjust accordingly.
— *Chen Shou: Records of the Three Kingdoms*

One may triumph over one weaker than oneself,
but if both are equal then weakness may win and its
strength is immeasurable.
— *Liu An: Huainanzi*

The softest can move freely within the hardest and the
formless can enter the spaceless.
— *Ibid.*

Notes on Sources

Analects: See *Confucius*.

Bai Juyi (772 – 846): Realist poet of the Tang dynasty and one of China's greatest poets. An outstanding candidate in the imperial examinations, he became an official and later a Hanlin Academician. Bai Juyi wrote his treatise *The Forest of Stratagems* (*Ce Lin*) in 806, early in his career as an official. At the age of 44, following the production of a volume of satirical poems, he was demoted and exiled from court on the grounds that his outspoken comments on the assassination of the prime minister had usurped the functions of the official hierarchy. He was later reinstated but finally sought a provincial post where he earned a reputation as a sympathetic and effective administrator, particularly in the field of irrigation.

Ban Biao (3 – 54): Historian of the Eastern Han dynasty and father of the historian Ban Gu (q.v.). Given an official post by the Han emperor Guangwu on the recommendation of General Dou Rong whose adviser he had been, but later resigned due to ill health. Ban Biao started the *Book of Han*, which was completed by his son Ban Gu and daughter Ban Zhao.

Ban Gu (32 – 92): Historian and poet. His *Book of Han (Han Shu)* was the first to rearrange existing material chronologically by dynasty. It covered a period of 230 years and set a pattern which later histories followed.

Bao Zheng (999 – 1062): Scholar, author and much-praised official who served during the reign of Emperor Renzong of the Northern Song dynasty. He refused office in order to look after his elderly parents. He returned to the capital after the death of his parents and was appointed imperial censor and later Prefect of Kaifeng, a politically sensitive post where he added to his reputation for incorruptibility. He has a reputation as a symbol of justice even today.

Book of Changes (Zhou Yi): An extremely early manual for divination by the use of the Eight Trigrams *(Ba Gua)*.

Book of Later Han: See *Fan Ye*.

Cao Xueqin (c.1715 – c.1764): Novelist and author of the colloquial novel *Dream of the Red Chamber (Hong Lou Meng)*, a work which was ten years in the writing and which realistically describes life in a wealthy but increasingly corrupt and licentious Chinese household. It has been translated many times. Perhaps the best English translation is that of David Hawkes (and later John Minford) under the novel's alternative title the *Story of the Stone (Shi Tou Ji)*.

Cao Zhi (192 – 232): Younger brother of Cao Pi who became ruler and then king of the state of Wei despite their father Cao Cao's initial preference for Cao Zhi. His later poetry reflects the grief and resentment that he felt at his situation. He is also credited with being the originator of Buddhist chant in China.

Chao Yuezhi (1059 – 1129): Scholar and official.

Chen Chun (1159 – 1217): Philosopher of the Southern Song dynasty. In his later years a disciple of Zhu Xi (q.v.).

Chen Liang (1143 – 1194): A disputatious philosopher and poet of the Southern Song dynasty. He advocated a form of realism in government. Imprisoned twice on the basis of false allegations, he died before he could take up the official post to which he had been appointed.

Chen Shan: Song dynasty scholar of the mid 12th century.

Chen Shou (233 – 297): Historian and military official who started writing his history of the kingdoms of Wei, Shu and Wu, the *Record of Three Kingdoms (San Guo Zhi)*, in 280. It recorded events of the previous 60 years. Subsequent historians have regarded it with respect but as not without personal bias.

Chen Zi'ang (659 – 700): Able official who wrote knowledgeably of the political and military problems of the western border regions, a political reformer and (conservative) poet who fell out of favor, resigned and died in rural isolation at the age of 41. Regarded as a better poet than politician.

Cheng Hao (1032 – 1085): Educator and philosopher whose teachings, with those of his close associate Cheng Yi (1033 – 1107) formed the Rationalist school of Neo-Confucianism.

Cheng Yi (1033 – 1107): See *Cheng Hao*.

Classic of Poetry (Shi Jing): Also known as *The Book of Songs*. The earliest collection of Chinese poetry and song, dating from the 11th to 6th centuries BC. It comprised court odes, folk songs and chants for sacrificial ceremonies together with other material, 305 items in all.

Compendium of Five Lamps (Wu Deng Hui Yuan) (1252): Compiled by the monk Pu Ji of the Song dynasty. A Zen text ascribed to the Lingyin Temple near Hangzhou.

Confucius (Kongzi) (551 – 479 BC): Philosopher and founder of one of the principal schools of Chinese philosophy. Often mentioned in the same breath with his disciple Mencius. The *Analects (Lun Yu)*, also known as the *Analects of Confucius*, is regarded as a record of the sayings and opinions of Confucius and his disciples, as well as of the discussions they held. Written during the 5th to 3rd centuries BC, it is the fundamental work of Confucianism and continues to exert a strong influence on Chinese and East Asian thought and values.

Cui Dunli: Scholar and writer of the Southern Song dynasty (1127 – 1279).

Cui Xian (1478 – 1541): Ming scholar appointed to the Hanlin Academy who, despite his abilities, was demoted or posted to the provinces several times during his career either because of the power of the court eunuchs or because he fell out of favor with the emperor.

Cui Yuan (77 – 142): Scholar, official and calligrapher noted for his running script.

Dai Zhen (1724 – 1777): Qing dynasty official and literary figure of wide scientific interests who criticized Neo-Confucianism and regarded the individual as paramount. He is considered one of the pioneers of scientific study in China.

Debates on Salt and Iron (Yan Tie Lun): See *Huan Kuan*.

Deng Xi (545 – 501 BC): Thinker and reformer who believed that the rule of rite should be replaced by the rule of law and produced his own manual of punishments. *Deng Xizi* is considered to be a record of his sayings and opinions.

Dong Zhongshu (179 – 104 BC): Western Han dynasty philosopher and scholar who expanded the principles of Confucianism into a theory of government.

Du Fu (712 – 770): Tang realist poet who also followed an official career. One of China's best known and greatest poets.

Du Guangting (850 – 933): Daoist scholar, philosopher, poet, calligrapher and novelist who pursued an official career but spent his later years in hermetic contemplation at Mount Qingchengshan one of the original centers of Daoism. He wrote one of the earliest martial arts short stories and two poems where the number of characters in each line increased by two every line from the original two to 28 and 30.

Fan Jun (1102 – 1150): Scholar, official and philosopher.

Fan Ye (398 – 445): Historian and imperial official. He fell victim to intrigue, did not complete his history, the *Book of Later Han (Hou Han Shu)* and was executed together with many of his family.

Fan Zhongyan (989 – 1052): Northern Song official and soldier who was several times the victim of intrigue because of his outspoken views. Recalled to service in 1040 after the establishment of the Xixia dynasty on the North West frontier, he was dispatched to the border and found the Song frontier garrisons, after 30 years of peace, defective in organization, logistics and strategy and incapable of winning the border war. Following Xixia successes, he stabilized the border with fortifications and garrisons (notably Dashuncheng) and a policy of generosity towards border tribes.

Fang Bao (1668 – 1749): Qing official and essayist who was implicated in the publication (he wrote the preface) of a book regarded as inflammatory, whose author, Dai Mingshi, was impeached. Fang Bao was condemned to death and spent several years in prison but continued to write. He was eventually released after the death of the Emperor Kangxi and pardoned. Several hundred people were caught up in the case which achieved some notoriety.

Fang Xiaoru (1357 – 1402): Well known Ming scholar.

Fang Yizhi (1611 – 1671): Philosopher and scientist who became a Buddhist monk after the fall of the Ming dynasty in 1644 and organized an underground movement aimed at the restoration of the dynasty.

Feng Menglong (1574 – 1646): Novelist and dramatist. *Stories to Caution the World (Jing Shi Tong Yan)* is a reworking of existing material. He reworked two other books *Illustrious Words to Instruct the World (Yu Shi Ming Yan)* and *Stories to Awaken the World (Xing Shi Heng Yan)*.

Fu Xuan (217 – 278): Scholar, official and poet. In 268, he advanced five proposals for improving agriculture and the life of the peasants in order to cope with the floods and famine of the time.

Ge Hong (c.281 – 341): Daoist scholar and theorist and famed seeker of the elixir of life or pill of immortality. After appointments as an official became a hermit on Mount Luofu in the northern part of Guangdong province.

Gu Yanwu (1613 – 1682): A Neo-Confucian polymath who contributed to many fields of learning. He played a part in resistance to the invaders as the Ming dynasty collapsed and is regarded as one of the pioneers of learning during the Qing dynasty.

Guan Yin Zi: A Daoist work, said to have been written by Guan Yin at the the end of the Spring and Autumn period.

Guan Zhong (? – 645 BC): Also known as Guanzi. Statesman of the early Spring and Autumn period.

Guo Xiashu: Poet of the period of the Three Kingdoms who dedicated five poems to the philosopher and musician Ji Kang (q.v.).

Guo Zuo (c.448 – 515): Scholar and official under the Northern Wei dynasty whose talents led to rapid promotion. He promoted the assimilation of northern nomad tribes to Han culture. He was ennobled for his role in the planning of the removal of the capital from Datong to Luoyang and became an imperial adviser.

Guoyu: An early historical work which takes the form of a compilation of court records and other material from the Zhou dynasty between 990 and 453 BC. Its authorship has been a matter of dispute but has been ascribed to Zuo Qiuming of the early Spring and Autumn period. Its principal characteristic is a concentration upon historical personages.

Han Fei (c.280 – 233 BC): Legalist philosopher. His collected writings *(Han Feizi)* were assembled posthumously. Some have been translated in Burton Watson (1964). *Han Fei Tzu: Basic Writings*. New York: Columbia University Press. A complete translation by W. K. Liao (London: Arthur Probsthain, 1939) is available online.

Han Ying: Poet and official of the Western Han dynasty and the originator of a poetic form to which he gave his name.

Han Yu (768 – 824): Scholar, poet, highly regarded essayist and official whose early career was somewhat chequered. He advocated centralized government and opposed the Tang dynasty system of devolved provincial governorships. As an orthodox Confucian his political views were complicated.

Hong Zicheng (1573 – 1620): Also known as Hong Yingming, a late Ming writer of whom little is known. *Vegetable Roots Discourse* (*Cai Gen Tan*) contains a section on the art of self cultivation and combines elements of Confucian, Daoist and Buddhist thought. There are many translations of this quaintly named work. The author spent some time as a hermit.

Hu Hong (1106 – 1162): Southern Song philosopher of the Rationalist School who, despite never holding an official post, devoted as much energy to matters of state as to scholarship.

Huainanzi: See *Liu An*.

Huan Kuan: Han dynasty official. *The Debates on Salt and Iron (Yan Tie Lun)* is his account of the proceedings of an imperial conference in 81 BC which examined the problems of the supply of salt and iron. It was the first systematic treatment of the problem.

Huang Tingjian (1045 – 1105): Poet and calligrapher of the Northern Song dynasty and founder of the Jiangxi style of poetry. He was a pupil of Su Shi (q.v.), with whom his name became associated as "Su-Huang."

Huang Zongxi (1610 – 1695): Son of a father who sought to impeach one of the court eunuchs, was imprisoned and subsequently died of ill treatment. He was praised for the way in which he sought posthumous justice for his father. Like many Qing scholars he was interested in astronomy and mathematics. His calculations, based on the occurrence of solar eclipses, cast some doubt on the previously accepted dating of major historical works.

Huangfu Shi (c.777 – c.835): Tang official and literary figure, pupil of Han Yu (q.v.).

Ji Kang (223 – 262 or 224 – 263): Author, poet, Daoist philosopher and musician of the period of the Three Kingdoms.

Ji Yun (1724 – 1805): Scholar and official. Also known as Ji Xiaolan and "Tobacco Pouch Ji" because of his addiction to tobacco. He was chief editor of the *Complete Library in Four Branches (Si Ku Quan Shu)* a selection of over 3,000 titles made for the imperial library, a process which began in 1771.

Jia Dao (779 – 843): Tang dynasty poet, who started life as a monk and later returned to secular life. Tradition has it that a poem of his complaining about a curfew on monks brought him to the attention of Han Yu (q.v.) with whom he subsequently studied.

Jia Yi (200 – 168 BC): Political theorist and imperial adviser *(Bo Shi)* at the age of 21. Died of grief and remorse at the age of 33 after his ruler was killed in a riding accident.

Li Ao (772 – 836): Tang dynasty philosopher, essayist and official. Pupil of Han Yu (q.v.) whom he assisted in promoting the ancient literature movement. He wrote an account of a trip to the South, *Coming to the South (Lai Nan Lu)* which has some claim to be one of the earliest diaries.

Li Bai (701 – 762): Famous Tang dynasty poet. A literary prodigy as a child he was born and brought up in north-west China. He had an interest in martial arts and spent his early manhood travelling. He was employed for a while at the Hanlin Academy but was forced to leave the capital for political reasons. He later became an associate of the poet Du Fu (q.v.) in Loyang. He was caught up in the events of the An Lushan rebellion in 756 and exiled but pardoned en route. His later life was one of some hardship. His travels gave him a sympathy for the sufferings of the people which was reflected in his poetry. His poetry has been described as filled with the spirit of romanticism.

Li Baiyao (565 – 648): Tang dynasty historian who completed the official history of Northern Qi, the _Book of Northern Qi (Bei Qi Shu)_, started by his father Li Delin.

_Li Er_: Known as Laozi. One of the principal Chinese philosophers and founder of the Daoist school of philosophy of the Spring and Autumn period; author of the _Classic of Morality (Dao De Jing)_, which describes the Dao as the mystical source and ideal of all existence: invisible, but immensely powerful; the root of all things.

Li Gang (1083 – 1140): A Song dynasty military official renowned for his resistance to the Tatar (Jin) hordes and his (largely unheeded) strategic advice.

Li Qingzhao (1084 – c.1151): Song dynasty poet and one of China's greatest women poets. Her father was a well known scholar and her early life was lived in some luxury. She and her husband (who later died) were both art collectors and were forced to flee to southern China by the troops of the invading Jin dynasty. Her early poetic style was one of elegant restraint but after the death of her husband her poetry reflected the sadness and hardships of her life.

Li Qunyu: Tang dynasty poet whose poems met with imperial approval. The short poem *Releasing Fish* (*Fang Yu*) is regarded as having profound philosophical significance.

Li Ruzhen (c.1763 – c.1830): Qing dynasty writer and novelist. *Flowers in the Mirror* (*Jing Hua Yuan*), a novel of fantasy, rather resembles *Gulliver's Travels*, but with fairies. It is the source of the phrase "let a hundred flowers bloom" (*bai hua qi fang*).

Li Zhi (1527 – 1602): Ming dynasty scholar and official. He was imprisoned on a false accusation and later committed suicide.

Liang Qichao (1873 – 1929): Scholar and journalist, one of the leaders of the reformist movement of the late 19th and early 20th centuries. The fluency of his written style contributed to the modernization of literary forms. He was also extremely politically active but spent his later years teaching and writing.

Liang Zhangju (1775 – 1849): Qing dynasty civil and military official and writer.

Lie Yukou: Known as Liezi, Daoist philosopher of the early period of the Warring States. He advocated *qing* *jing wu wei*, a passive view of life which emphasized the natural order.

Lin Bu (967 – 1029): Reclusive naturist poet of the Northern Song dynasty. He lived as a hermit on Mount Gushan by Hangzhou's Western Lake where he spent time visiting temples by boat. On the arrival of guests his servant was instructed to release a crane to summon him home. He is reputed not to have visited a town for over 20 years.

Lin Zexu (1785 – 1850): Late Qing official and Viceroy of the Two Guangs (the provinces of Guangdong and Guangxi), he played a major role in resistance to western attempts to develop the opium trade through the port of Canton (Guangdong). Despatched to Canton in 1839 as Imperial Envoy with the task of suppressing the trade, he confiscated and destroyed the complete stock of opium held by British traders in their godown. Following the Opium War of 1840 he was blamed for the failure to defeat British military operations and was demoted and exiled to Xinjiang. His *Poem of Farewell to His Family* was written on the eve of his departure. He is regarded as a national hero.

Liu An (179 – 122 BC): Prince and scholar. Reputed inventor of *Doufu* (bean curd). The *Huainanzi* was a treatise which refined the essence of the Daoist philosophers before the Qin dynasty but included miscellaneous stories and legends as well as other material.

Liu E (1857 – 1909): Scholar and novelist prominent in research into the oracle bone fragments. His short satirical novel *The Travels of Lao Can (Lao Can You Ji)* attacked the corruption of the late Qing dynasty bureaucracy. It has been translated into English a number of times.

Liu Ji (1311 – 1375): Scholar, official and poet at the end of the Yuan dynasty and the beginning of the Ming. In later life he took service under the Ming as a military adviser and acquired a considerable reputation as a strategist, on a level with Zhuge Liang (q.v.).

Liu Shao (c.186 – 245): Philosopher of the period of the Three Kingdoms. His *Records of People (Ren Wu Zhi)* related the physical characteristics of the human body to the five Chinese elements: metal, wood, water, fire and earth. It also related this spiritual metaphor to the five constant Confucian virtues: Benevolence, Righteousness, Propriety, Wisdom and Fidelity.

Liu Xiang (c.77 – 6 BC): Lexicographer and official. His *Garden of Stories (Shuo Yuan)* was a collection of historical stories and legends with a commentary which promoted Confucian moral and political concepts.

Liu Xie (c.465 – 532): Known as Liu Bowen, scholar and official, but best known for his literary achievements, particularly *The Literary Mind and the Carving of Dragons (Wen Xin Diao Long)* an early major work of literary criticism.

Liu Yuxi (772 – 842): Tang dynasty philosopher, poet and official who became one of the central figures in the political reform movement led by Wang Shuwen (753 – 806).

Liu Zhiji (661–721): Tang dynasty historian who wrote the first Chinese commentary on historiography.

Liu Zhou (514–565): Writer. In *Liuzi* he outlined his ideas for government and the nurture of talent.

Liu Zongyuan (773–819): Philosopher, writer and official. Left over 600 works but his reputation rested on poetry. He suffered a number of demotions during his career. A good friend of Bai Juyi (q.v.).

Lu Jia: Writer, statesman of the state of Chu. Famed for his powers of persuasion.

Lu Jiuyuan (1139–1193): Southern Song dynasty philosopher, educator and founder of Neo-Confucianism School of Mind (*Xin Xue*).

Lu Shanji (1575–1636): Of Mongolian extraction and born into a distinguished family in Hebei province. He followed an official career mainly in the Hoppo (Hubu), one of the six Boards, which was broadly responsible for finance, commerce and customs.

Lu Shiyi (1611–1672): Scholar of broad interests and accomplishments who devoted himself to a life of secluded study on the fall of the Ming dynasty in 1644.

Lu You (1125–1210): Patriotic and prolific poet (more than 9,300 poems). Forced by his mother to separate from his wife, an event which influenced the rest of his life.

Lu Zhi (754–805): Enlightened and outspoken official to the Emperor Dezong who advocated policies that did much to prevent the collapse of his rule.

Lü Buwei (? – 235 BC): Statesman in the state of Qin. His *Lü's Spring and Autumn Annals (Lü Shi Chun Qiu)* is mainly a compilation of the writings of scholars before the Qin dynasty.

Lü Desheng (fl.1521 – 1566): A Ming dynasty writer. His *Words for Children (Xiao Er Yu)* was an updated collection of moralistic sayings designed to inculcate good behavior.

Lü Kun (1536 – 1618): A Ming dynasty thinker and official in the Board of Punishments. He wrote several books of which *Lamentations (Shen Yin Yu)* is one.

Lü Zuqian (1137 – 1181): Born of an illustrious official family he was more interested in scholarship than an official career despite his outstanding performance in the imperial examinations.

Luo Dajing (1196 – 1252): Song official. Although he held a number of provincial posts as a legal official he abandoned his career and devoted himself to literary criticism after being implicated in court intrigue and impeached. *Dew of Jade in the Forest of Cranes (He Lin Yu Lu)* includes notes and commentaries on poets of earlier dynasties.

Meng Ke (c.372 – 289 BC): Also known as Mencius. Disciple, at two generations removed, of Confucius. He advocated benevolent government.

Mo Di (c.468 – 376 BC): Founder of the philosophical school of Mohism which emphasized universal love on the basis of equality rather than social degree. He regarded war as a malady of his times. His work *Mozi* includes a section against war.

Ouyang Xiu (1007 – 1072): Song dynasty scholar, historian, poet and upright official. Political and literary reformist.

Pei Songzhi (372 – 451): Southern Song dynasty historian.

Pi Rixiu (c.838 – c.883): Poet and official of the Tang dynasty.

Pu Songling (1640 – 1715): Short story writer and essayist of the Qing dynasty. His fame rests mostly on his collection of short stories *Liao Zhai Zhi Yi*-translated into English as *Strange Stories from a Chinese Studio* by H.A. Giles (1845 – 1935) and more recently by John Minford.

Qi Jiguang (1528 – 1587): Ming dynasty military theorist and general who, by re-thinking tactics, organization and weapons eradicated Japanese piracy in the maritime provinces of east and south-east China.

Qian Qi (1467 – 1542): Ming dynasty official and poet.

Qu Yuan (c.340 – c.278 BC): Official and statesman of the state of Chu and one of China's greatest romantic poets. *Sorrow at Parting* (*Li Sao*) is a lengthy lyric poem of political content. It expresses the poet's feelings at the suffering he has endured and criticizes the state of the nation.

Record of History (Shi Ji): See *Sima Qian*.

Record of Rites Compiled by Dai De (Da Dai Li Ji): A compilation of the sayings and opinions of Confucian scholars before the Qin and Han dynasties. Believed to have been compiled by Dai De during the Western Han dynasty.

Record of the Hall of Beauty (You Mei Tang Ji): A piece by Ouyang Xiu (q.v.) in praise of a beauty spot near Hangzhou.

Recorded Sayings of Dahui Zonggao: Record of the sayings of a Zen Buddhist monk who lived from 1089 – 1163.

Shang Yang (c.390 – 338 BC): Political philosopher and minister of the state of Qin who advocated both measures intended to strengthen the Qin state and government of remarkable harshness and cruelty. In the end, he perished equally cruelly at the hands of his enemies—he was torn limb from limb. His legalist philosophy was recorded in *The Book of Lord Shang*.

Shen Dao (c.395 – c.315 BC): Legalist philosopher who taught in the state of Qi during the period of the Warring States.

Shen Deqian (1673 – 1769): Qing dynasty scholar and poet.

Shen Hanguang (1618 – 1677): Poet who brought up his two younger brothers after the death of his father, an official under the previous (Ming) dynasty.

Shen Juyun: Qing scholar.

Shen Kuo (1031 – 1095): An official of wide scientific interests who was sensitive to environmental issues. When governor of Yanzhou (today's Yan'an in Shaanxi province) he recorded the existence of oil whilst on campaign against Xixia incursions.

Shi Jiao (c.390 – c.330 BC): Legalist philosopher of the Warring States period and author of *Shizi*.

Shi Nai'an: Author of *The Water Margin (Shui Hu Zhuan)*, a collection of tales of derring-do based on the exploits of heroes of the past.

Sima Guang (1019 – 1086): Historian and essayist. Author of the first detailed and comprehensive Chinese historical chronology *Comprehensive Mirror to Aid in Government (Zi Zhi Tong Jian)*. It covered 1,362 years from 403 BC during the period of the Warring States. His political views were conservative.

Sima Qian (c.145 or c. 135 BC – ?): Historian and thinker. His *Record of History (Shi Ji)* covered about 3,000 years of Chinese history from the time of the mythical Yellow Emperor to 87 BC.

Sima's Rules of War (Sima Fa): A military treatise incorporating earlier works and compiled during the middle of the period of the Warring States by command of King Wei of Qi (356 – 320 BC).

Sorrow at Parting (Li Sao): See *Qu Yuan*.

Stratagems of the Warring States (Zhan Guo Ce): A well known historical work. The identity of the original compilers is not clear but it is believed to have been edited into one work by Liu Xiang (q.v.) during the final years of the Western Han dynasty.

Su Shi (1037 – 1101): Son of Su Xun (q.v.) and far better known as the poet Su Dongpo. The *Record of the Hall of Thought (Si Tang Ji)* was written at the invitation of a friend, a writer of *ci* (one of the forms of Chinese poetry), who believed in the significance of "Think before acting" and had erected a building dedicated to the idea.

Su Xun (1009 – 1066): Literary figure of the Northern Song dynasty. Known with two of his sons as "the three Sus" (see *Su Shi* and *Su Zhe*). A prolific essayist with reformist political views.

Su Zhe (1039 – 1112): Son of Su Xun (q.v.). Brother of Su Shi (q.v.). Northern Song dynasty essayist.

Sun Wu: A successful general and military theorist in the state of Wu. A version of his military classic, *The Art of War (Sun Zi Bing Fa)* written on bamboo slips, together with a similar treatise by Sun Bin, was excavated from a Han dynasty tomb in Shandong province in 1972. His writings have remained influential in military circles to the present day. The earliest reliable translation into English was that of Lionel Giles published in 1910. There have been many others since. Sun Wu stands head and shoulders above other theorists.

Tan Qiao: Daoist scholar of the Five dynasties (907 – 960), who spent some time as a hermit and sought the pill for immortality. *The Book of Transformations (Hua Shu)* is an important Daoist text which advances a view of the cycle of creation that starts from the Void and moves through Spirit and Essence to Form and then returns to the Void.

Tao Qian (365 or 372 or 376 – 427): Also known as Tao Yuanming. Poet and essayist. After several years as a magistrate and minor official he resigned his position and retired to rural solitude. His poetry mainly concerns itself with the hermetic rural life.

The Book of Lord Shang (Shang Jun Shu): A compendium assembled during the period of the Warring States which contained the views of the politician and Legalist thinker Shang Yang (q.v.).

The Constancy of Laws (Jing Fa): A work of the Huang-Lao school, thought to date from the period of the Warring States and excavated from a Han dynasty tomb in Changsha in 1973.

The Literary Mind and the Carving of Dragons (Wen Xin Diao Long): See *Liu Xie*.

The School Sayings of Confucius (Kong Zi Jia Yu): First mentioned in the *Book of Han*, it was thought to be a collection of sayings and opinions attributed to Confucius. The earliest surviving compilation is by Wang Su (195 – 256). Various versions of it have circulated over the centuries with long running disputes about its authenticity.

The Six Secret Teachings on the Way of Strategy (Tai Gong Liu Tao or Liu Tao): Also known as *The Six Bow-cases of Duke Tai*. An early and justly famous work on warfare and strategy. It has been well known outside China since at least the 16th century when it was known in Japan, and there have been translations into Japanese, Russian, German and English. There is an English translation by Ralph D. Sawyer.

The Spring and Autumn Annals of Minister Yan Ying: A description of the sayings and actions of the statesman Yan Ying (? – 500 BC). There are various views about its authorship.

The Yellow Emperor's Classic of Internal Medicine (Huang Di Nei Jing): Also known as *The Inner Canon of Huangdi* or *the Yellow Emperor's Inner Canon*. A very early and important medical (and Daoist) text.

Vegetable Roots Discourse (Cai Gen Tan): See *Hong Zicheng*.

Wang Anshi (1021 – 1086): Political thinker, literary figure and prime minister to the Emperor Shenzong in 1070. A political reformer, he memorialized the throne in 1058 seeking an improvement to a situation of "an accumulation of poverty and weakness" and the adoption of the Legalist policy of enriching the state and strengthening military power (*Fu Guo Qiang Bing*), a slogan which was also used during the Meiji restoration in 19th century Japan.

Wang Bo (649 or 650 – 676): Well known Tang dynasty poet.

Wang Chong (27 – c.97): Philosopher and official of the Eastern Han dynasty.

Wang Da (1368 – 1644): Ming dynasty author.

Wang Fu (c.85 – 162): Philosopher of the Eastern Han dynasty. A commentator who was critical of the corruption and avarice of the court at a time of social instability and natural disaster. The *Discourse of a Man Concealed (Qian Fu Lun)* was an acerbic political polemic written by a man who never sought office and lived in seclusion. Some passages in the book are still regarded as obscure.

Wang Fuzhi (1619 – 1692): Great scholar of the last years of the Ming dynasty. He took part in resistance to the Qing dynasty. In philosophy he summarized and developed the traditional Chinese theory of materialism—that matter precedes spirit.

Wang Tingxiang (1474 – 1544): Scholar and independent thinker who opposed rigid adherence to old forms merely for the sake of them. He had an interest in the natural sciences, especially astronomy and geography. He eventually achieved high office as Secretary of the Military Board in Nanjing.

Wang Tong (584 – 617): Philosopher and official who set up a private academy of more than one thousand disciples. *True Sayings (Zhong Shuo)* collects Wang's teaching and observations on the model of the *Analects of Confucius*.

Wang Yangming (1472 – 1529): Original name Wang Shouren. The name Yangming derived from his hometown Yangming Cave. Ming dynasty scholar, philosopher, educator and civil and military official. Raised severely by his parents who, angered by their son's reluctance to study and his addiction to chess, threw his chess set into a river. The son's response was this poem:

The chess set that was joy in passing days,
By mother cruelly tossed away.
Soldiers, pawns unsaved from the river flood,
Generals in formation drowned.
Torrent driven horses surge a thousand li,
Elephants downstream amid the river's wave.
The world trembles at the cannon's sound,
Zhuge Liang the sleeping dragon now awakes.

Wang subsequently modelled himself on Zhuge Liang (q.v.) the famous general and strategist and went on to suppress anti-dynastic peasant risings in south east and central south China. The influence of his philosophical teachings based on the Neo-Confucianism School of Mind (*Xin Xue*) reached beyond China to Japan and Korea.

Wang Bi (226 –249): Wei dynasty scholar of the period of the Three Kingdoms who belonged to a school of metaphysics which combined elements of Confucian and Daoist thought. Amongst his many works, the most well known are the *Commentary on Laozi* (*Lao Zi Zhu*) and *Commentary on the Book of Changes* (*Zhou Yi Zhu*).

Wang Wei (701? – 761): Poet, artist and musician. Known as the Buddha of poetry. Deeply influenced by the Zen School of Buddhism.

Wei Liaozi: A text on military strategy written by Wei Liao. One of the military classics of ancient China.

Wei Yingwu (c.737 – c.791): Tang dynasty naturist poet who also followed an official career. His poetry reflected a hankering after the pastoral life.

Wei Zheng (580 – 643): An Imperial Censor under the Tang dynasty. An orthodox Confucian who believed in the Confucian virtues rather than the efficacy of severe punishment as a means of government.

Wu Jing (669 or 670 – 749): Tang dynasty historian and official. *Outline of Affairs during the Zhenguan Reign of the Tang Dynasty (Zhen Guan Zheng Yao)* is a major source of material on imperial and ministerial conversations, memorials and prescripts in the period of the Tang emperor Taizong (599 – 649).

Wu Qi (? – 381 BC): Military theorist on a par with Sun Wu. *Wuzi* is the only surviving part of a longer *Wuqi* written in the early Warring States period. *Wuzi* developed Sun Wu's principles of war.

Xu Gan (171 – 218): Poet, philosopher and literary figure of the Eastern Han dynasty.

Xue Xuan (1389 or 1392 – 1464): Neo-Confucianist scholar and official who followed in the footsteps of Zhu Xi (q.v.).

Xun Kuang (c.313 – 238 BC): Known as Xunzi. Thinker, educator and literary figure of the state of Zhao. He travelled widely and criticized and developed the ideas of the pre-Qin philosophers on the basis of his own Confucian views. He did not share Meng Ke's (q.v.) view that humanity was basically virtuous and believed that the natural order proceeded under its own momentum and not at the behest of man.

Xun Yue (148 – 209): Easter Han dynasty philosopher and historian from a poor family who could memorize at sight and was able to recite and explain the *Spring and Autumn Annals* as a child. *The Mirror of History (Shen Jian)* attacked the use of divination to form policy and advocated a number of other reforms.

Yan Yanzhi (384 – 456): Literary figure, poet and official with service as an infantry officer. A close friend of Tao Qian (q.v.). Some critics regard his poetry as rather artificial and a little lifeless.

Yan Yuan (1635 – 1704): Educational theorist who criticized established educational practice. He believed in the paramount importance of fostering talent.

Yan Zhenqing (708 – 784): Official and noted calligrapher whose life came to an end when he was strangled by a rebellious general. Two years later the general was murdered by his own subordinates and the rebellion came to an end.

Yan Zhitui (531 – after c.590): Official. His educational views, which were Confucian, were influential. *The Family Instructions of Master Yan* (*Yan Shi Jia Xun*) was the first comprehensive and systematic educational manual in China. Based on Yan's personal experience its scope extended beyond family education to history, literature and ethics. His personal life was eventful.

Yan Zun: A hermetic scholar of the Western Han dynasty who refused official preferment and earned his living by divination. Once he had earned enough for his daily needs he returned to his study of Laozi.

Yang Shi (1053 – 1135): Philosopher, scholar and pupil of Cheng Hao and Cheng Yi (q.v.).

Yang Wanli (1127 – 1206): Scholar, official and poet. Frequently memorialized the throne on topics such as the needs of defense.

Yang Xiong (53 BC – 18 AD): Poet, linguist and scholar who overcame the disability of a stammer to win imperial favor on the basis of his poetic gifts. He wrote the first Chinese lexicon of dialects.

Yao Chong (650 – 721): Tang dynasty official who served as Prime Minister under three reigns—Wu Zetian, her son Emperor Ruizong, and her grandson Emperor Xuanzong.

Ye Mengde (1077 – 1148): Song dynasty poet. He pursued a career as an official and lived as a hermit in his later years.

Yuan Cai (? – 1195): Scholar, official and gazetteer, his only surviving work is *Yuan's Hereditary Rules (Yuan Shi Shi Fan)* on family morality and relationships.

Yuan Mei (1716 – 1798): Successful provincial official and poet and essayist with a large following. Resigned his position at the age of 33 (or 40) in order to look after his widowed mother. He restored a dilapidated property in Nanjing and lived there for nearly 50 years. Apart from poetry he also wrote two popular collections of tales of the fantastic and a cookery book published in 1792.

Yuan Zhen (779 – 831): Tang dynasty poet and official. He was an associate of Bai Juyi (q.v.) with whom he advocated the adoption of a new poetic form first proposed at the beginning of the Tang dynasty by the poet Du Fu (q.v.).

***Yue K*e** (1183 – c.1242): Song dynasty scholar and official. The *Court Tales (Ting Shi)* is an account of the activities within and without the Northern and Southern Song court. Its style is close to that of a novel.

Zeng Guofan (1811 – 1872): Controversial late Qing dynasty statesman, minister and military figure. In 1853 he raised an army in his home province of Hunan and took the field against the rebels of the Taiping Movement, basically a peasant rising which was suppressed over the next ten years. *Letters of Zeng Guofan to His Family (Zeng Wen Zheng Gong Jia Shu)* on the proper conduct of households, appeared after his death and is more a manual of behavior than a guide to domestic administration.

Zhang Jiuling (673 or 678 – 740): Scholar, official and poet of the Tang dynasty.

Zhang Shunmin: Northern Song dynasty official and poet.

Zhang Xuecheng (1738 – 1801): Thinker, historian and historical critic with a particular interest in local histories and historical methodology.

Zhang Zai (1020 – 1077): Northern Song dynasty philosopher and one of the founders of the Neo-Confucian rationalistic School of Principle (*Li Xue*). His texts were required reading for candidates in the imperial examinations during the Ming and Qing dynasties.

Zhao Chongguo (137 – 52 BC): Western Han dynasty archer, cavalryman and general. Active in the North West in campaigns against the Xiongnu. *On the Twelve Advantages of Military Farms (Tiao Shang Tun Tian Bian Yi Shi Er Shi Zhuang)* emphasized the function of garrisons in stabilizing areas occupied by nomadic tribes thus avoiding the expense of maintaining an army in the field.

Zheng Xie (1693 – 1765): Artist, calligrapher and poet. Either side of an official career he lived in Yangzhou. One of the Eight Masters of Yangzhou.

Zhou Shouchang (1814 – 1884): Qing dynasty scholar, official and poet who played a prominent part in the actions to suppress the Taiping Rebellion of 1851 – 1864.

Zhou Xingsi (469 – 521): Official and courtier. The *Thousand Character Classic (Qian Zi Wen)* contains 1,000 characters in groups of four which describe nature and the life of man without using each character more than once. There is, in fact, one repetition so there are actually only 999 characters. Tradition has it that the text was written overnight at the command of the emperor and that by morning the author's hair had turned white.

Zhu Bailu (1617 – 1688): Qing dynasty educator.

Zhu Shunshui (1600 – 1682): Alternative name of Zhu Ziyu. Civil and military official and philosopher in the latter years of the Ming dynasty who took part in resistance activities against the incoming Qing dynasty. On the final collapse of the Ming he fled to Japan and then to Annam. Despite the stringent regulations prohibiting the entry of foreigners, the Japanese scholar Ando Seian (1622 – 1701) was later able to secure a living for him in Nagasaki and Edo (later Tokyo) where he taught for more than 20 years. His Neo-Confucian philosophical teachings had considerable influence in Japan.

Zhu Xi (1130 – 1200): Southern Song dynasty Confucian scholar, educator and founder of the school of Neo-Confucianism.

Zhuang Zhou (c.369 – 286 BC): Also known as Zhuangzi. Early Daoist philosopher of the Warring States period.

Zhuge Liang (181 – 234): Famous strategist, general, statesman and inventor of the period of the Three Kingdoms. Zhuge Liang believed that there were nine qualities required of a successful general and eight faults to be avoided. He invented the wheelbarrow and remains a central character of Chinese historical films.

Zuo Qiuming: Or Zuoqiu Ming. Historian of the Spring and Autumn period in the state of Lu. His chronicle of events *Chronicle of Zuo* (*Zuo Zhuan*) covers the period c.722 – 464 BC.

Zuo Si (c.250 – c.305): Poet of the Western Jin dynasty. Of unprepossessing appearance and by nature retiring he moved to court when his younger sister was taken into court. He was active in literary circles.

Dynasties in Chinese History

Xia dynasty	2070 BC – 1600 BC
Shang dynasty	1600 BC – 1046 BC
Zhou dynasty	1046 BC – 256 BC
Western Zhou dynasty	1046 BC – 771 BC
Eastern Zhou dynasty	770 BC – 256 BC
Spring and Autumn period	770 BC – 476 BC
Warring States period	475 BC – 221 BC
Qin dynasty	221 BC – 206 BC
Han dynasty	206 BC – 220 AD
Western Han dynasty	206 BC – 25 AD
Eastern Han dynasty	25 – 220
Three Kingdoms	220 – 280
Wei	220 – 265
Shu Han	221 – 263
Wu	222 – 280
Jin dynasty	265 – 420
Western Jin dynasty	265 – 316
Eastern Jin dynasty	317 – 420
Northern and Southern dynasties	420 – 589
Southern dynasties	420 – 589
Northern dynasties	439 – 581
Sui dynasty	581 – 618
Tang dynasty	618 – 907
Five dynasties and Ten States	907 – 960
Five dynasties	907 – 960
Ten States	902 – 979
Song dynasty	960 – 1279
Northern Song dynasty	960 – 1127
Southern Song dynasty	1127 – 1279
Liao dynasty	916 – 1125
Jin dynasty	1115 – 1234
Xixia dynasty	1038 – 1227
Yuan dynasty	1279 – 1368
Ming dynasty	1368 – 1644
Qing dynasty	1644 – 1911